Where's The Fire

Michelle Graham

Published by:
Rays of Hope
PO Box 336, Angwin, CA 94508
Phone: 707-965-9400

Edited by Sylvia Kalua and Charity Glass
Cover Design:
Artist–Arnol Jiminez
Graphic Artist–Tyson Thorne
Photographer–Dave Sherwin

Where's the Fire?

ISBN 0-9658766-3-2
1. Religion 2. Youth

This book is dedicated to:

The Pathfinders

and to my friends Tonya and Audra
who have made seeking God the center of their lives.

Special Thanks to:

God, for being so awesome that we will study your character for eternity and still have more to learn.

Roland, for your reading and re-reading and your wonderful encouragement.

Justin, for your enthusiasm and patience.

Gavin, for your patience and support.

Mom, for your hours of reading and editing and for your ideas.

Dad, for your research and guidance. You knew how to challenge me to make it better.

Bobby, for your inspiration and for the original concept.

Kim, for your support and enthusiasm.

Chet, for your support and encouragement.

Dick, for going to bat for us and for being a great role model. Also thank you for the inspiration for the last chapter.

Lindsey, for your evaluation and encouragement.

Larry, for your support.

Contents

Forward

*"And we know that the Son of God
has come and has given us understanding
so that we may know him who is true."*
1 John 5:20

I read the manuscript and am deeply touched and impressed. The book uses a narrative method to describe the difference between the altar of Cain and the altar of Abel. This method—speaking through the lips of Adam, Cain, Abel and others, does a wonderful job of maintaining interest while teaching the truths of Salvation and personal responsibility.

What I like best about the book is that it speaks the gospel so clearly to young minds. It is an excellent book!

Dick Duerksen, World Youth Leader

The Old Man

The sun shines brightly this morning above the rich green hue of the grass that carpets the gently sloping hills. I shuffle along at a snail's pace, stopping frequently to rest and catch my breath. I am bent over with age and can no longer walk in the easy stride of my younger days.

I have lived a long life and though it has been full of pain and bitter disappointment, it has been a story of the truest love. My life's story is a beautiful song, strong and sweet with the purest of melodies.

My beloved wife was laid to rest years ago, but I find that I think of her quite often . . . she was gorgeous . . . .

* * *

"Come, my love, I want to tell you about my day," I would say to her. She would come and sit in my lap so I could tell her my story, then she would tell me hers. It wasn't because we didn't know the story—we had spent the day together. Rather, it was to recount for each other our feelings, disappointments, and hopes.

On one particular day I called her to me. It was a strange day for I had been away from her for several hours. I had taken our two young sons for a walk so I could talk to them man to man. My wife had not gone with us because I wanted to spare her the pain of the experience. I felt I needed to talk with my sons alone. I needed to tell them the plain and simple truth as I had understood it. My wife listened eagerly and intently to my story.

"You knew I woke the boys early this morning didn't you?" She nodded. "Well, when I woke them, they were eager for an adventure and asked, 'What is it Dad? Where are we going?'"

I had a difficult time looking them in the eyes because I knew what kind of adventure was in store for them.

We walked with the sun rising behind our backs. Along the way, I picked up a little white lamb from the flock of sheep and carried him in my arms. He was a beauty and I didn't get very far with him because the boys wanted to take turns carrying him.

"Dad, why are you bringing Sky?" one of them asked.

"What do you mean . . . Sky?"

"This little lamb's name is Sky."

"You named him?" I felt sick and unsure of how I would get through my talk.

My wife's eyes opened wide and she gave a little cry but quickly covered her mouth and I continued my story.

I led the boys to the Place of Remembrance. Naturally all they saw was a pile of stones. They started to climb on the rocks and I had to ask them to get down. They took one look at my face and got down in a hurry. They seemed to sense that I was in a serious mood. I didn't know what else to do, so I started right in.

"Your mother and I were banished from our home," I said while pointing toward the gate that barred the way.

"We already know that, Dad." The boys looked at me as if it was a very boring subject.

"Yes, you know part of the story, but I haven't told you all of it. I wanted to wait until you were old enough to understand the whole thing."

The boys looked at each other and smiled their secret smile. "You know how they look at each other out of the corner of their eyes and smirk?" My wife nodded, grinning. I grinned, too, just thinking of our boys. We had so much fun together watching the two of them as they grew. Well, anyway, I continued talking to them as if I hadn't noticed their little smile.

I told them, "When your Mother and I ate from the Tree of Knowledge of Good and Evil, we were disobeying God." They both nodded and I continued. "We knew we were disobeying God but we didn't understand what would happen to us if we ate one little piece of forbidden fruit. God told us that if we ate that fruit, we would die but we didn't really know what *die* meant."

"What happened?" Cain asked, shifting his weight from one foot to another.

"What happened to me?"

"Yeah, what happened to you, Dad?" Cain asked, nodding.

"I ate a piece of that fruit and felt great for a minute. But then all of sudden I felt afraid. I had never been afraid before."

"Wow," Cain whispered, "then what happened?"

"I ran. I probably haven't run that fast ever again."

"Why did you run—who was after you?" Abel squeaked.

"I heard God walking in the garden. He was looking for your mother and I. We were terrified so we hid from him."

"What did God do to you?" Cain wanted to know.

"Was he mad?" Abel asked, his voice still squeaky.

"No, God wasn't mad. He had come to the garden in the evening like he always did. He came to spend time with us but we were hiding. He called and called our names and when he finally found us, he held out his arms. Your mother and I could see that he wasn't mad and after a moment of hesitation, we went to him. He wrapped his great big arms around us and cried. We all cried together. Then he led us out of the Garden and this is where we live now."

"Will God ever let us go back to live in Eden?"

"Yes, Cain, we will return to our home, but not right away."

We all turned to look toward the gate where one of God's shining angels stood blocking the way into Eden.

"Why not? Why can't we live in there?" Cain asked, forgetting about the large blade of grass that he had wound around his hand. I noticed that his fingers were turning purple so I stooped to unwind the grass. As I did, I explained, "Leaving our garden home helped me to understand that your mother and I were in trouble."

When I said that, both boys gasped and said, "Trouble! What kind of trouble?"

"When I disobeyed God I was turning away from him. I turned away from God because I thought I could do things my way. I learned later that doing things my way, without God, leads to trouble . . . big trouble."

My beloved Eve stopped me at this point in the story and asked, "Adam, why didn't you blame me? I was the one who ate that fruit first and you know it."

"Sh-h, Honey, this is my story. You must be patient with me; you will have your turn." I patted her knee and she smiled softly, then asked, "Would you like a drink?"

We shared a drink of cool water flavored with mint leaves before settling down to continue with my story.

After I told the boys that trusting my own way instead of trusting God was trouble, then Cain wanted to know, "What's wrong with relying on yourself?"

"Everything is wrong with that—everything. If you trust yourself then you don't think you need God. And unfortunately, that's exactly what I did. I didn't believe what God had told me. I thought I knew best so I ate the fruit.

Cain was upset. "Why didn't God keep you from doing that?" His eyes seemed to deepen in color and almost looked as if they flashed.

"What do you mean, flashed?" Eve interrupted me again.

"I don't know. It was like he was upset with God or something. It surprised me because I've never seen him look that way before. Now it worries me. I'm not sure what he thinks about all of this," I told her.

"Well, don't worry, Darling, just keep talking to him and I will talk to him, too," she reassured me with her comforting smile.

I nodded and then said, "Okay, where was I . . . ? Oh yes, Cain wanted to know why God didn't keep me from disobeying."

I told Cain, "God will never force his love on anyone—it is a gift. God had tried over and over again to explain to me what would happened if I trusted myself—I would close my heart to him and become a completely different person. God knew that my loving heart would be damaged and I would become evil and die."

Cain still seemed upset and interrupted me, "Why didn't he stop you?"

"God will never take away anyone's choice from them. He created us free and because He loves us so much, we remain free to choose whether or not will accept his gift of love."

"But Dad," Cain said with an urgency in his voice, "God loved you—you were his creation. Wasn't there anything he could do? I just don't understand why He put that tree in Eden in the first place?"

My beloved Eve sniffled. I looked at her and saw that tears were brimming in her eyes. I didn't want to hurt her. She had already been through so much pain. Some days she carried her guilt around with her like a huge rock. I told her to rest. "We will finish later if you wish." Then I held her in my arms while she cried. After a time she fell asleep. I thought my heart would burst with her pain.

I held her for a long while, feeling her warmth. When the sun sank low in the sky I gently laid her down and stood to welcome the night. The stars slowly twinkled into the night sky. I watched them and thought of my wife's tragic pain. I wondered if I should finish telling her my story. I wanted to tell her because I had learned so much by trying to teach our sons.

"I am ready now." My wife's voice broke through my thoughts. I turned to smile at her. We ate some sweet fruit together. "Hmm, where was I?" I mumbled when we had finished our meal.

"Cain was asking you why God put the tree of Knowledge of Good and Evil in Eden," Eve said helpfully.

Oh, yes, . . . well, I told them, "Before God created your Mom and I, he was the Creator of many angels in Heaven. One of his angels stopped believing that God cared about everyone's happiness. The angel made up his own ideas about who God was. He began to believe that God always wanted to be in charge and was forcing a lot of unneeded rules on the angels. He let the ideas grow in his heart until it broke up his friendship with God."

"How did it wreck his friendship with God?" Cain asked.

"The angel was so suspicious that he stopped trusting God. Everything that God did to win his trust back was twisted in his mind. Doubts filled every thought. His distrust of God's goodness grew stronger and stronger. Finally, he became God's enemy." The boys looked at each other in astonishment as I continued.

"God put the tree in Eden to protect me."

"How did it protect you?" Cain asked.

"God could have allowed his enemy to talk to me anywhere, but he didn't. He said the angel could only talk to me from one place—the Tree of Knowledge of Good and Evil. You see, God didn't just make us free—he made the angels free, too."

"Oh, I see," Abel grinned. "God let the angel talk to you because God gave him freedom to think and to share his ideas. Because of his freedom God let him in the garden, but to protect you, he could only be in one tree and not everywhere."

"That's right, Abel. Do you understand, Cain?"

"No, I still don't understand why you had to leave Eden."

6

"I had to be separated from my perfect home because I had chosen to see and experience evil—it was the result of *my* choice."

"Oh," said Cain. "If God let you right back into the Garden, you wouldn't know that you were in trouble."

"And you wouldn't know that the trouble was that you trusted yourself instead of God," Abel added.

"That is right."

Cain still wasn't satisfied with my answer. "If being sent out of your home was a lesson about disobeying God, then what does *die* mean?"

That was the reason I had taken them to the altar but I wasn't ready to show them the answer yet. We were having such a special moment that I wanted to talk with them a little more. "Die is what happens when we are separated from God and won't accept his help."

Cain got a scared look on his face and wanted to know, "Are we separated from God?"

My wife squeezed my shoulder. She saw the tears in my eyes and wanted to comfort me. I covered my face in my hands and wept. She wept with me.

"I know, my love, I know," she soothed.

"It was so hard . . . so hard telling them that I, their own Father, had gotten them into all this trouble with distrust and separation from God. I lost God's love in my heart and they were born with the changes that had happened inside of me. They were born with my selfish, rebellious spirit."

"*Our* rebellious spirit, you mean. I know it was difficult, Adam, but you had to—you just had to tell them the truth."

"It was a terrible moment in their young lives, Eve," I sobbed, "and it was a terrible moment in mine, too."

She let me cry and then pried my hands away from my face. I looked up into her eyes. What I saw there made me feel as if I could fly through the sky like a bird, trilling a song of love and thanks to my God. In spite of it all, Eve was still in love with me. "Thank you, God," I whispered. "Continue," she said. I nodded and wiped my face.

I was trying to tell the boys it was my fault that they had been born with a terrible legacy. Their hearts did not naturally love God. I had a hard time talking through the tightness in my throat. After swallowing the lump that had formed there, I said, "Cain . . . Abel, that is what I chose for myself and you. I chose to trust myself and now the act of turning away from God is a natural part of your hearts."

"What is going to happen to us?" Abel asked.

"God is going to help us."

"He is?" Cain asked.

"Yes, God is going to give us his own Son who will help us out of the trouble we are in."

Cain asked, "Is he going to die?"

What could I say? I had to tell him, "Yes, his Son is going to die for *us*."

"How does he help us if he dies?" Abel asked.

"He is going to show us what God was talking about when he said, 'If you eat from that tree you will die.'"

"Why?" Cain asked.

"So that we will be able to understand what will happen if we resist his help."

"God is going to do that for us?" Able asked.

"Yes."

"Why?" Cain wondered.

"Because he loves us."

"That's incredible!" Abel said.

"Come boys, I want to show you something."

"What?" they responded together.

"I'll show you, but first we need to gather some tree branches."

8

Cain and Abel made a game of it. They ran here and there picking up sticks from below the trees, laughing. Sky, the little lamb bounded after them.

"Is this enough, Dad?" Cain asked, smiling. He had so many sticks that he was dropping them everywhere.

"Yes, we have plenty now, thank you." The boys added their branches to my pile and we put the wood on the pile of stones. "This is an altar," I said pointing at the stones. Then I picked up the lamb, Sky. They were very quiet and Abel looked worried.

I put my hand on Sky's little head and talked to God.

"God in Heaven, You are my Father and I need you. I need you to destroy the spirit of rebellion that I have allowed in my heart. I know it was my choice to trust myself and because of it, I often feel my heart fighting against your love. I don't want this terrible legacy for my family. Please recreate us. Thank you for this little lamb who can help us understand your love."

I wiped a tear from my eye and told the boys to place their hands on the lamb. Their prayers touched me deeply and I fumbled awkwardly for the knife in my clothing. Abel started to cry out, but I quickly slit the lambs throat as he watched me in stunned silence. The warm red life poured out of the lamb. I watched Cain and Abel struggle against the tears that sprang into their young eyes. I laid the lifeless body of the lamb on the altar.

"This is die," I whispered, ". . . this is die."

The boys stood in silent amazement at the deed I had just done. I could see them struggling to understand and they soon broke down and wept. Abel gave me a look that I will never forget. I felt as if the knife had pierced my heart.

"What kind of a look was it?" Eve asked, sensing my pain.

"It was a look of complete horror and sorrow."

Then Cain looked at me and sobbed, "I don't understand."

9

"You will in time," I said, putting my arm around him and lifting him into a hug. Then I gently lowered him to the ground and told Abel to join us. The three of us knelt by the altar and I prayed, *"God in heaven, please forgive and heal us from sin and separation from you."*

Suddenly fire flashed from heaven. With wide eyes the boys watched as the fire burned up both the lamb and the wood that was on the altar. After a few moments, Abel turned to me and asked, "What was the fire for?"

"It means that God is pleased with the sacrifice," I said.

I looked again at my wife. She looked at me. "Is that the end?"

I shook my head, "I don't think so . . . I am not sure they understand."

"It will take time," she said, caressing my face with her hand.

* * *

I remember her touch on my face. It was as soft as if a butterfly had gently brushed up against my cheek. As I stand here leaning on my stick, I remember how naive we were. We had no idea what choice Cain would make. He misunderstood God and brought heart-rending grief down upon Eve and me. I miss her so much . . . my heart aches for her companionship. That is why I find myself standing here daydreaming about her.

I know that I am about to lay down my weary bones in rest, for I have grown very old. I am 930 years old. I no longer view death with fear because I am tired. These eyes have seen so much pain and misery that I welcome the rest. But before I rest, I want to warn you about two altars—altars that at first seem alike, yet are very different. Search for the difference. Find the truth that Abel found and Cain rejected.

A Bitter Conflict

Plunk . . . plunk . . . plunk . . . ripples extended from each pebble as it dropped into the water. It was a quiet day along the shores of the river and I sat where it went out of its course just far enough to make a quiet pool. Something had gone terribly wrong and I was feeling frustrated and lonely. I half-heartedly threw pebbles into the pool and listened to the sound of them hitting the water.

I wondered about the morning and the events that had taken place. I knew that everything was changed and I feared that the change would be forever. I had been searching for something different but now that I had found it or *it had found me* I wasn't so sure I was happy about it.

I had always been adventurous and often traveled across the meadows and valleys and climbed the highest hills to discover remote, exotic places. I loved sleeping out under the stars and waking at dawn. I relished the feel of wind through my hair and sun on my face. I had always traveled knowing that I could return home to love and friendship. But now I was unsure.

As I returned home from my latest adventure I anticipated a joyful reunion. I was not disappointed—my parents were excited to see me and the close bond that I had with my brother seemed the same as always. But this morning had been different and I knew that nothing would ever be the same again. I sighed and threw another stone into the water. Tears suddenly welled up in my eyes as I stood up and coughed. What had I done to make things go so wrong?

I paced along the shore thinking back to another time when my heart had been troubled and I had come here to think.

I remember it was the morning after my Dad had killed my favorite lamb. He had taken my brother and me to learn about offering a sacrifice to the Creator. My heart was aching and I missed my little lamb, Sky. I started feeling mad at my Dad for killing my lamb. I felt guilty for my bitterness. I didn't want to be mad and I tried very hard not to be, but the feeling just grew inside of me. My anger grew worse and worse every day until I was furious. I spent a few days brooding over my anger until finally one morning I found myself stumbling along the little path toward the place where Dad had built the altar. I fell on my knees beside the stones and poured out my heart to God. Then the most wonderful thing happened. The more I talked to God about the way I was feeling, the better I felt. I stayed there for a long time and didn't realize I had fallen asleep until I awoke to my brother's voice.

"What are you doing sleeping here?" He was smiling at me in amusement.

I yawned and stretched. When I looked up at my brother he offered me a hand. I took it and stood up noticing that it was late in the afternoon.

"How long have I been sleeping here?"

"I don't know. Mom sent me to find you so we could eat together."

"Oh . . . okay, thanks."

"What were you doing here anyway?"

"I came to talk to God."

"Oh . . . ?"

"Yeah, and I feel great!" I said, jumping up to touch a branch that was just out of my reach. "I was mad when I first got here. I asked God to help me—to change me."

"And did he?"

"Yes, He did. Isn't that incredible?"

"You look the same to me," my brother shrugged.

I rolled my eyes at him and ran toward home. Of course he ran, too, and soon passed me, laughing all the way.

That afternoon when I found myself praying at Dad's altar I began to understand God's power to change me. My anger was totally gone. I still thought about my lamb, Sky, but it was different. I felt grateful for what his death had taught me about God. I was glad that Dad had chosen a lamb that was special to me so I could understand how God must feel about giving up his own son. I learned more from Sky than any other creature I have ever loved.

I know God changed my angry feelings. In place of anger he gave me thankfulness and love. I know I'm not the one who changed my feelings because that's what I had been trying to do.

There had been a troubling conversation with my older brother, too, not long after the death of Sky. I was sitting up in a tree right here by the river one afternoon when he came running. "There you are!" my brother yelled. "Do you want to go in for a swim?"

I wiped my face and shrugged, "Okay."

We had a great time jumping, diving and swimming in this pool. We laid out in the sun soaking up the warmth and drying off. I was just looking up into the sky, watching the clouds and enjoying my own thoughts when he broke into my daydreams.

"I've been thinking."

"About what?" I asked, feeling lazy in the warm sun

"About God and his Son dying and all of that." I waited to hear what he was going to say.

"God moved our parents out of their home, but Dad doesn't really seem to understand why."

"What do you mean?"

"Well, Dad said that he had to leave Eden because he trusted himself."

"Yeah."

"That isn't the real reason."

"It's not?"

"No. They had to leave because they were bad and ate the forbidden fruit. They can't return until they are good again. Don't you see? They made God angry and now they can't go back to their home until they make peace with him and prove that they can obey."

"But Dad said that God wasn't mad."

"God was mad or else he wouldn't have made them leave Eden. They have to obey and then they can move back home."

"Isn't that what Dad said about going back to Eden?"

"Yeah, sort of, but Dad thinks that he was in trouble before he ate the fruit. He also thinks that he can't be good. Did you hear him when he said we naturally turn away from God?"

"Yes?"

"Well, that means our hearts are bad. If we were born bad then why is it so easy to be good?"

"I don't know."

"I can be good."

"Yeah, I know."

"So here's what I'm thinking: if I can prove that I can be good and obey God, then I should be able to live in Eden."

"I don't know. What do we do about the condition of our hearts?"

"We can overcome our bad hearts. We can make ourselves good if we really want to."

"So you don't think we need God's Son to help us?"

"I'm just wondering about it all. If I can already obey then I don't see a need for anyone to die."

"I don't know."

"Well, it was just a thought."

We didn't talk about it any more after that and I wondered who was right. I didn't think Dad would lie to us. He had always worked very hard to tell us the truth, even when it hurt.

Soon after I noticed my brother and I spent less and less time together. He loved to grow a garden and spent hours amidst his plants but I enjoyed caring for the sheep. As a shepherd I learned many things about God's wonderful love. Roaming around the countryside caring for sheep I began to understand God's methods of teaching us about himself. I learned about God's patience while taking care of the lambs. I learned about God's power when I watched the sun rise and felt the heat on my face. I realized that God was listening to us all the time when I looked up into the night sky and pondered the stars. I found that I could go to God anytime, anywhere, just by talking to him—I could even talk to him in the middle of a meadow. When I cleaned and dressed a wound on one of the sheep I learned about God's desire to heal me inside. I realized that God never leaves me alone to over come my selfishness and impatience. He was just waiting for me to let him recreate my heart.

In looking back I can see I have learned many things in my travels but one thing I didn't realize until today was how different my brother and I have become. For one thing we differ in our communication with Mom and Dad. I relish long talks while he likes to keep it short.

As a result of his short conversations I'm not sure my brother understands some of the things that I have learned.

I remember one of my favorite long talks with my mom. I was sitting in a large tree when she climbed up beside me and sat swinging her legs. "How are you?" She had asked me.

"Fine, Mom."

"No, what's bothering you? You have been quiet lately." She always seemed to know when I was upset about something.

"I'm a little confused." I paused, trying to figure out how to explain myself. "If you were a branch and God was the tree, then was leaving Eden like being broken off from the tree?"

My mom looked at me, blinking, then said, "Yes, I guess you could say that."

"Then who broke you off the tree?"

"I guess I broke myself off."

"But Mom, didn't God make you leave Eden?"

She nodded, "yes."

"I don't understand."

"It's simple, . . . when I broke myself off, I began to die. I didn't want to die, but I couldn't repair the damage I had done. It was then that I knew I needed help—God's help. This was the lesson I learned by leaving Eden. It was the lesson that made me ready to accept God's plan to help me."

I nodded and then smiled. "You know, Mom, I've been trying to figure that out for years."

"So have I."

"Really?"

"Yes. It has taken me a long time to understand why God sent us out of our home."

"He did it so you would feel a loss, didn't he?"

"Yes, Abel. That's the only way we would ever admit to ourselves that we needed anything." Tears filled her eyes.

I reached for her hand and held it. "I'm glad God does whatever it takes to help us." She nodded, then sighed. We sat together in the tree until dusk.

Another day my Dad came and stood at the base of a tree

I was sitting in and called me down. He said he wanted to talk about something important so I climbed down where he was. He explained that a day had been set for my brother and I to take our own sacrifices to God. A sinking feeling came over me as I listened and from that time on I looked forward to the day with mixed feelings. I dreaded the day because I would have to kill a lamb, yet I looked forward to it because I was eager to learn more about God.

Well, the day finally arrived. Today was the day and with mixed feelings I knelt in prayer early this morning and asked God for strength and understanding. Then I walked across the fields and found a perfect lamb. I carried him to the place where my Dad had built an altar. The lamb rode happily in my arms and I found myself talking to him. "Well, little guy, you are the one. You are going to help me today." I sank my face into his sweet, soft wool feeling guilty about where I was taking him.

When I arrived in the clearing near my Father's altar of stone, I set the lamb down. He seemed content to lay beside me while I worked. First, I dug up twelve stones and tried to build an altar but they kept toppling over. The task was much more difficult than I had expected. I had to dig up a lot more than the twelve stones my father used to get my altar together.

A short time later my brother arrived and called, "Hey!"

"Hey, yourself."

He came over to see what I was doing. "Did you dig up all of those?"

"Yes," I said, laughing. "It's a lot harder than it looks to get these stones stacked in a solid shape like Dad's altar."

"Well, I guess I better give it a try." He walked a short distance away from me and started digging.

I finished my altar first and picked up my lamb. I was glad that my brother had gone far enough away that he couldn't hear me pray. I wanted to be alone with God. *"God, I am a sinner. I feel totally unworthy to come to you but I am glad that you accept me into your presence. I want you to recreate me to be just like You. I want to be filled with your love all the time. Please forgive me for the desires of my selfish heart."*

I picked up my knife from the stones and shuddered. *"I don't have the strength to do this . . . , God help me,"* I whispered. I held the knife to the lambs throat as I looked into the beautiful eyes of the innocent little victim. "I can't do it," I sobbed lowering the knife.

Glancing toward the angel that stood by Eden's gate I saw that he was watching me and noticed that a tear was running down his cheek. I wondered if he was crying *for* me or *with* me.

Turning back to my sacrifice I clenched my teeth, gripped the knife and quickly slit the lamb's throat. I watched in horror as the lamb's red blood ran out of it's body and it writhed in pain. I was suddenly sick and wretched.

Watching the lamb die and feeling his warm blood on my arms, I caught a glimpse of myself. I saw how horrible my heart was, how selfish. I wondered how I hadn't seen my utter wretchedness before. I wondered how I had gotten so bad, but then I remembered that God loved me and promised to heal my wretchedness and make me into a new person.

With hope in my heart I placed the lifeless body of the lamb on my altar and bowed my head to pray. *"God, my Father, thank you for who you are. You have shown me the truth about my heart and how much it is offended by your love. My heart keeps wanting to drag me farther and farther from you. Save me, Father. Please save me from . . . from . . . myself. And thank you, thank you so much for giving your Son to save all of us. Amen."*

I had hardly breathed the last word when fire exploded on

the altar. I fell to the ground and shielded my eyes with my arm. The fire was so bright that I could hardly look at it, but as I did I knew that I was forgiven.

When the sacrifice was totally gone, I stood up and looked at the smoking stones. I wondered what God meant by sending fire to burn up the lamb. I knew that it was God's solution to the problem of our mistrust, but I didn't know how.

I closed my eyes and replayed the whole thing in my mind. Then I realized that God was declaring his willingness to get rid of the spirit of selfishness that was a natural part of me. I had felt the war within me—wanting to do the right thing but not being able to. *"Please send a fire into my heart and burn out the evil that is there. Create a new, clean heart inside of me so that I will be in harmony with you. I want to do the right things naturally."*

When I opened my eyes I felt calm inside and peaceful. I was sure that God was beginning his work in me already. It was wonderful to know that God could be trusted to change us into his friends.

Being lost in thought I was oblivious to my brother's preparations nearby. When I heard the sound of shouting, I turned to see what was going on and saw that my brother was shaking his fist toward heaven. Something must have gone terribly wrong.

Taking a few steps toward him, I watched. I had seen my brother angry before, but the look on his face was horrifying. I had never seen a look like that before and I felt my jaw drop. Without thinking about it, I took a few steps closer and saw the reason for my brother's terrible anger. There was no fire on his altar and I realized that there was no lamb, either. Then, I knew my brother's heart was locked in a terrible battle. His heart was fighting for it's independence and freedom from God's love.

19

"Don't do it," I whispered. "Don't fight God." I was standing there staring intently and praying for my brother when he turned and looked right at me. I broke from my intense concentration and looked away. It wasn't right for me to intrude on his private time with God, but my heart longed to help him.

I was about to say something but he turned back to his altar. I continued watching in agony as I saw him struggle. I finally walked up behind him and said, "What happened to your lamb? Why didn't you bring one? Without a lamb you can't understand what God is trying to teach us."

"Don't tell me what to do, little brother," he answered, keeping his back to me.

"I'm not trying to . . . it's just that I learned the most incredible thing about God changing us . . . and I had to kill a lamb to learn it."

"I'm here to thank God that I am a good person. I don't need to be changed."

"But we all need to be changed—you know that. Dad told us we were born bad . . . remember?"

"You think you're so smart. What makes you think I don't remember what Dad told us . . . do you think I'm stupid?"

"No, you know I don't think that. I just think God has been so merciful to our parents. He could have let them die, but He didn't. Instead His own Son is going to die."

"You call that merciful?" My brother was starting to yell. "No one should have to die so we can go back to Eden. Mom and Dad shouldn't have been sent out of there in the first place . . . it was their home . . . our home."

"You . . . you don't mean . . . what you're saying."

"Don't I?" Cain responded, still keeping his back to me.

"No, I know you better than that. I know you love God and want to obey Him. Why are you feeling stubborn today?"

"You think you know me, little brother?" he whirled around and yelled in my face. I blinked hard.

"I've known you all my life." I tried to smile at him but the smile didn't seem to help.

"Well, you know I'm not a bad person. Why does God love you more than He loves me?" he yelled.

I was shocked. I didn't know what to say. "He . . . , God doesn't . . . how could you say that? . . . He loves all of us."

"Really? . . . Than why isn't he happy with my sacrifice? I brought him the very best of my garden. Why isn't my best good enough? Why is he so unreasonable?"

I didn't understand how it could have happened but my brother seemed to be mad at God.

"But God said to bring a lamb. Just thanking God can't teach us about our hearts. God chose the lamb to teach us a lesson about what will happen to us if we don't let God change us. God wants to change us. Don't you believe that?" I felt sick inside.

"I can see that God has chosen you as his favorite over me," my brother said, turning away.

"God would never prefer me over you . . . I'll talk to you later when you aren't so mad. If you will just ask God to take your anger away, I know He will. He's done it for me many times." I turned sadly away and ran not wanting to intrude any longer.

I ran to the river and was soon throwing in pebbles. As I paced along the bank I knew that my relationship with Cain had changed forever. Maybe I was wrong to talk to him about it, but how could I not?

I wondered if there was anything I could do to help my brother. Surely he understood that God was a God of love. Why wasn't he letting God change his heart? God loved him so much. I loved him. I hated seeing him so angry and miserable.

Cain's voice interrupted my thoughts.

"Abel, Where are you?"

Turning from the river I called , "I'm over here," as I waved to him.

"Come, let's go for a walk."

"Sure." I wondered if he was still mad at me. I didn't mean to upset him. I had just wanted to help, but somehow I knew I had hurt him more deeply than I could comprehend. It would have been worth making him angry if only he could understand how wonderful God is. His love had changed my life. I knew it could change my brother's, too.

"Cain, I'm sorry if I made you mad," I told him. "I love you."

I knew when I said it that I would do anything . . . anything to help him.

He suddenly spun around to face me. I was horrified at what I saw and just stood there frozen in my tracks. Then I saw him raise his hand in the air . . . .

Where's the Fire?

"They keep moving farther and farther away from us," said a tall, thick man in a gruff voice.

"We can't do anything about it," a smaller man said.

"I think we can," I said. The five men turned toward me, startled, as I stepped forward to join them. They hadn't seen me standing in the shadows of a large Cypress tree. The men greeted me with nods and smiles. One of them even bowed slightly.

"What can we do?" the tall man asked. I smiled at them and wondered if they were the ones I should share my plan with. I had been stalking these five men for weeks, along with other rebel groups. They were not the most ruthless men of the city, but rather the most secretive and careful. I wondered if they were smart enough to appreciate the depth and simplicity of my plan.

The five men listened intently to my ideas and nodded in agreement. They saw the brilliance of the plan and were wise enough to know that it was better than waging an all out war. After thanking me for sharing my idea and promising to meet again so we could plan further, they bowed and disappeared into the forest.

I stood for a moment reflecting on what I had just shared with the men and shuddered. What I was planning was horrific. As I was standing there thinking, I was startled by a sound off to my right. I tried to look in the direction of the noise without turning my head. I held my breath to listen, but my heart pounded in my ears.

After a moment I saw a movement and breathed a sigh of relief.

"Hey!" I said gruffly.

"Oh . . . Grandpa," the young boy whined, as he crawled

out from under a bush, "you always know it's me." He smiled and I grinned at the boy fondly—he was becoming so grown up.

"What were you doing in the bushes?"

"Nothing," he said, looking at his feet.

"Nothing eh?" I tried to smother a smile.

The boy shook his head then looked up, "I was spying!"

"Yes, I can see that, but why?"

"I'm practicing to be like you."

I couldn't help smiling then. He was my favorite grandson. He reminded me of myself when I was young.

"So, now that you are here, what shall we do?"

He hesitated for a moment. "Well, I was wondering about something, Grandpa."

"Oh? What were you wondering about?"

"I heard something when I was little and I have been wanting to ask you about it for a long time."

"And you waited until now? . . . You have a pretty good memory . . . What do you want to know?"

"Well . . . I was wondering if . . . I, um . . ."

"What is it, boy?"

"Did you kill your brother?" His words tumbled out in a rush.

I cleared my throat. "Who told you that?"

"I don't remember . . . it was a long time ago."

"It doesn't matter . . . but why do you want to know that?"

"I don't know . . . did you kill him?"

I nodded.

"When?"

"When I was your age." His eyes opened wide and he drew in a sharp breath. I wondered if he was afraid or impressed.

"I remember the day clearly," I said, and began my story.

* * *

24

My feet were wet because the dew was heavy on the ground. I was walking along a path I had worn through the valley forest just east of my home. After a short walk I left the valley and climbed to the top of a hill—my hill—when the light of dawn was just beginning to streak across the sky. It was the day that I had been looking forward to for quite a while.

"What day was it?" my grandson asked, interrupting me.

"It was the day that had been set aside since before our births for my brother and I to make the choices of a man."

"What are you talking about?"

"I'm talking about a rite of passage—a sign of manhood."

"Oh."

"It was a ceremony that declared our independent choices about how to solve the problem that exists between God and man."

"Wow, am I old enough to do it?"

"Yes, you are old enough, but we don't perform the ceremony in our city."

"Oh . . . ," he looked disappointed.

"Our relatives living in the distant hills still perform the ceremony, but we know better."

"What do you mean?"

"That ceremony can destroy a young man's belief in himself."

"How?"

"When you go through the ceremony you have to acknowledge that you are weak and need something besides your own strength. If you perform the ceremony relying on your own will power, you get rejected."

"Rejected?" The boy had a look of shock on his face reminding me of his father.

I nodded and was just about to continue my story when we both heard a slight rustle in the leaves a short distance away.

I pointed toward the bushes and my grandson silently disappeared.

*   *   *

I stood alone for a short while, listening. I was able to make out the direction of soft footsteps approaching. I turned in that direction and watched, but soon heard footsteps coming from another direction and then another. I guessed it must be the men returning.

Shortly, five men appeared from the shadows.

"Sir,"one of them addressed me, bowing low, "We have taken your suggestion to our elders and they agree."

"Excellent," I smiled.

"When do we begin?" one of the men asked, trying to hide his eagerness.

"As soon as you find the women."

"That may take a considerable amount of time," the largest man of the group said in his deep voice.

"Let us throw a celebration, then."

"What kind of celebration?" the large man asked, his eyes betraying his interest.

"Let's call it a celebration of life and you can scout out the most beautiful and cunning women of our city."

The men smiled and agreed. They bowed and left quickly, anxious to get on with the plans for a city wide celebration.

My grandson reappeared looking anxious.

"What was that all about?"

"Oh, we're planning a little party, but we can talk about it later. I was telling you a story . . .

"Yes, you were telling me about the day that you were to become a man. The day you killed your brother.

"Oh yes . . ." I said, continuing my story.

* * *

I was standing on the hill where I spent time every morning at sunrise. I always walked out there because I wanted to get my day started right. I remember bowing myself to the ground and praying:

"Dear God, thank you for the new day and for all the blessings you have given me. Thank you for life, strength and wisdom. I am about to become a man and I want you to know that I will do all I can to solve the problem between you and my family."

"What exactly was the problem between you and God?"

"My father had disobeyed God. That meant that I was born disobedient and I needed to earn God's forgiveness and try to win His love and acceptance."

My grandson had a puzzled look on his face, but I ignored it and went on.

After my prayer I stood and watched the sun rise in the sky. As I did I thought about my parents and the pain they had suffered because of their disobedience. I wanted to be able to achieve God's acceptance for myself and show my father how it was done. See . . . I had been working on the problem for many years—since I was a young boy. I believed my father's good deeds and humble attitude had not pleased God because that was all my father did. He did exactly what he had been told and then he waited for God to solve the problem. The way I figured it, God was waiting for my parents to use their own wisdom to come up with a solution.

"What do you mean?"

"Let's look at it this way. If you disobeyed your Dad and he sent you to your room, what would you do?"

"I would say I was sorry and run to my room."

"What would you do while you were in your room?" I

27

watched my grandson's face as he tried to wrestle with the problem.

After a moment he said, "I would think of ways to try to make up for what I had done wrong."

"What kind of things could you do?"

"I would promise not to repeat the mistake and I would offer to do something for my Dad that would make him happy."

"Exactly," I smiled, "That's what I was thinking about. I wanted to give God something more than he had asked for. I thought that if I gave up something that was important to me, it would be worth more. Especially if it was something that I had worked hard for."

"That seems logical."

"I thought so. I just had to figure out what to offer God."

That was the question I was pondering as I watched the sunrise. When I finally left my hilltop, the sun was climbing higher and the dew was starting to disappear. I went back along the path toward my garden, picking some palm branches along the way to weave a large basket. When I got to my garden I plucked some grapes to eat while I made the basket. Then I carried it through the rows, selecting some of my favorite fruits and vegetables. I was going to offer them as a gift to God.

"You decided to offer God food?" my grandson asked, with disbelief in his voice.

I nodded. "Yes, I was a master in the science of training plants and the beautiful food was the result of my hard work."

"Oh."

I didn't wait for any more questions, but continued.

There was a clearing in the trees just outside the east gate of my parents first home where I went to offer my gift to God. When I walked into the clearing, my brother was already there beginning his ceremony. I walked a short distance away from him and set my basket down so I could find some stones.

I set to work digging. When I had twelve large stones, I piled them carefully to form an altar. Stopping to rest, I glanced over at my brother. He was crying—he had killed a little lamb to present to God on his altar. I stood watching for a moment, then turned my attention back to my task.

"Why did your brother give God a dead lamb?"

"That's what God had asked for. It was an appropriate gift since my brother was a shepherd." I continued my story.

I piled wood on my altar and arranged the food very carefully. I wanted to be sure that everything was perfect before I offered it to God. When I was satisfied with the arrangement, I smiled and was just about to kneel in prayer when a bright flash of fire burst from the sky down onto my brother's altar. It was very exciting to see the bright flash and the flames. I turned away from the fire and with anticipation in my heart, I knelt in front of my altar. I can still remember my prayer:

"Dear God up in Heaven, I have brought you a gift. I am excited that I can bring a better sacrifice than a lamb. I have thought this over very carefully and since I am a plant trainer I have brought you a gift resulting from my hard work. It makes sense to me and I know you will like it. Please accept my ability to solve problems and send the fire like you promised."

I waited, . . . nothing happened.

"Nothing happened?" The boys eyes were wide in surprise and shock. I shook my head.

"What did you do, Grandpa?"

"Well, I remember turning to look at my brother and I saw that he was watching me."

"Was he spying on you?"

"Yes, he was spying on me."

"That's terrible, he had no business doing that.".

"I know," I said and then continued my story.

I waved him away but he didn't leave. Instead, he took a few steps toward me. I turned away from him and focused on my gift for God. Looking up toward the sky I said, *"Great God up in Heaven. Do I need to bring more fruit? I don't think any more will fit on top of this altar. Please accept this offering and send down your fire."*

I glanced at my brother one more time to see if he was still watching me . . . .

"Was he?"

"Yes. And when I looked past him I saw that the angel who guarded the gate of my parent's first home was watching me, too."

It wasn't any of their business."

I looked at my grandson and a sudden sadness gripped me. He understood my story perfectly and felt the same way I did. I wondered if he was doomed to the same misery I had experienced in my life. I shook the thought from my head and continued.

When I saw that my brother wasn't leaving, I was very uncomfortable. I looked toward heaven again and asked, *"God are you listening? I asked you to send fire. I am a believer in you and I have brought you a gift that I had to work hard for."* But God didn't answer. As I stood there waiting, I could feel my face getting hot.

"What happened?"

"I stood there feeling betrayed."

"I don't understand how God could treat you that way. You weren't trying to make yourself happy—you were trying to do something to make him happy."

"I know. I was trying so hard to get God to accept my way of doing things, but he didn't."

"God never sent any fire down on your altar?"

30

"No, and I even tried harder to get him to listen to me."

"You did? Why was God's acceptance so important to you?"

"God's acceptance of me meant that I would be given special privileges. I was supposed to have a special connection with God, since I was the oldest son."

"Oh, I see," my grandson nodded. "It sounds like God was giving your privileges to your younger brother."

I nodded, "That's exactly what I thought when God sent fire on my brother's altar and not on mine."

"So what did you do, Grandpa?"

I stood at my altar for a minute feeling confused. I wondered what more I could do for God. I felt like I was doing more than I had been asked to do. I couldn't figure out why God wasn't sending fire so I yelled, "Where's the fire?!!!"

Still there was no answer from the sky. I was embarrassed and angry. I thought God should have more respect for someone who was trying to make Him happy.

"Look at all I have done for you," I screamed. "You owe me God." Then feeling desperate I lowered my voice. "God, it looks to me like you are giving my privileges to my little brother. Well, I won't let You." I shook my fist toward heaven.

I was so angry and my brother had the nerve to walk right up behind me to say that he knew what was wrong with my sacrifice. I didn't need him to tell me anything. I already knew everything I needed to know—God loved my brother more than he loved me. I shut out the sound of my brother's voice. I hated him for coming between God and me and I whirled around to hit him, but he was gone.

"Why are you angry?" God's voice startled me.

"He talked to you?"

"Yes He did."

"Why are you so mad?" God asked, "I'm waiting for you to

understand that you cannot fix the problem between us—that's my job. My desire is not for gifts and offerings. I want your heart but you are keeping it from me by doing things your own way. You are allowing your heart to be controlled by a spirit that is at war with my love. I don't love your brother more. I love you and I want to save you from the unhappiness that you will find when you reject me. Why won't you let me heal the damage in your heart? Please, let me save you."

I knew God was right, but I was angry. I didn't like being treated like a child. I didn't understand why God had to be so stubborn. I wanted him to accept my offering. I didn't want him to change me.

I left my altar and walked back to my favorite hill. I didn't kneel because I didn't think God would listen. I stood and thought. The longer I stood there thinking about the way that my brother and God had treated me, the more my anger grew. Soon, my whole body was shaking and I couldn't stand it any longer. I had to do something so I ran to find my brother.

I found him by the river and called him to walk with me. He followed me back out to my hill. Along the way we were silent and my anger started to drain away until he said something. Then the anger welled up inside of me again more fierce than before. I turned around and looked at him. I felt no brotherly love; no fondness for the boy who had always been my best friend. I smashed my fist into his head, but it didn't relieve my anger. When I looked at his bloodied face I saw someone who was trying to get into my position next to God. I was the older brother and he was supposed to be next in line—not in front of me. I hit him again but it only seemed to feed my anger so I hit him again and again and again.

"Did your brother hit you back?" my grandson asked.

"No, it was really strange—he just took the beating."

The next thing I knew, my little brother was lying on the

ground—dead. I looked down at him and terror gripped me. I ran over the hill away from my home. I ran until I couldn't run any longer; then I collapsed next to a stream.

"What have I done?" I sobbed into the dirt. "What have I done?"

I spent the night there by the stream. The next morning I saw my brother's blood on my hands. It was dried on so I bathed in the stream. Even though I washed the blood off, the feeling of terror didn't leave me. I crouched under a bush all day, but nothing happened. After spending several days hiding in the shadows, my terror began to subside. One evening when the sun was sinking in the west, I crawled out of my hiding place to find something to eat.

I was picking some berries when God called my name. I scrambled to find a place to hide but it was too late. "Where is your brother?" God asked me. I was terrified so I lied to cover up what I had done.

"I don't know. . . Am I in charge of my brother?"

"What have you done? The voice of your brother's blood is crying to me from the ground."

I wondered if God was giving me the chance to tell him the truth but I couldn't admit what I had done. I was afraid—I thought God would send fire down from heaven and kill me, but he didn't. Instead he said, "You will no longer be able to grow and train plants because the earth has swallowed the blood that you shed. Instead of being a tender of plants you will be a wanderer."

When God said that I would no longer be able to train plants, I was angry. How could he separate me from the one thing that I loved to do. It wasn't fair! "My punishment is more than I can bear," I screamed. "You have driven me out of the land I love and away from your presence. I will be homeless . . . I will be a vagabond. Whoever finds me will kill me."

Then God answered, "If anyone kills you, vengeance will be taken out on him sevenfold." God marked me to warn anyone I met about God's vengeance so that they wouldn't kill me.

"I wondered when you got that mark."

I was tired of the story and wanted to talk about something else. After a few minutes of silence the boy seemed to understand how I was feeling so he changed the subject.

"The plan you are making with those five men is a good one, Grandpa."

"What plan?"

"You know, . . . your plan to break up God's relationship with your relatives . . . the ones who live far away in the hills? You know just what to do to get them to reject God. Sending our most beautiful women to their camp will make them forget about their God."

I took a deep breath and interrupted the boy.

"Young man," I said, "I want you to stay away from those men. They are not the kind of people you should be spending time with. Do I make myself clear?"

He nodded.

"And as for the rest of that crazy notion you have in your head, . . . well . . . you can forget about it." I looked sternly at the boy who simply nodded his head. I cleared my throat and sent him off to play. Then I walked out of the forest after him.

I was not all together unhappy about my grandson's discovery of my plan. He was a smart young man and would make good use of the information. I smiled to myself as I thought about the people who lived in the city—my city. Their only knowledge of God was what I had taught them. They were boldly defiant and I felt great satisfaction in the knowledge that through their rebellion I was taking out my own vengeance on God. I only wished I could do more. If I could, I would tear God from His throne and kill Him, just like I did Abel.

The Contest

The sun rose hot over the horizon for what seemed like the millionth time, showing the withered landscape. The trees stood naked against the dust and sand having shed their leaves long ago. River beds were dry and pond bottoms were cracked and coated in thick layers of dust. I was worried as I looked out over the brown hills that were barren of the life they had once sustained. I knew starvation threatened the few remaining livestock that roamed the countryside.

I stood looking out the doorway of my tiny home at the cursed and desolate country. Squinting against the light I noticed a lone figure walking southward through the choking clouds of dust with a purpose. The figure was that of a man dressed in rough clothing common to a specific line of work. When he got closer I could see that his black eyes glistened and his tanned brow was wrinkled in a look of determination. He stopped from time to time to sip from his water skin and wipe his brow. But he always returned to his southerly course without question or hesitation in his step.

"Someone's walking across the desert," I said turning away from the door. I walked across the dirt floor of my home and sat down heavily.

"We're going to die," I moaned softly.

"We must pray harder," my husband said meekly from the corner of the hut where he sat on a cot.

"We have prayed. The whole nation has prayed and look what it has gotten us—starvation and death." My husband only looked at me. He, too, was tired and hopeless. Anger flared up in my chest as I thought about what this strong, proud husband of mine had been reduced to from lack of work or purpose.

"How could the giver of life, that we worship so faithfully, hold a whole nation responsible for the defiance of one man?" I wondered aloud.

"I don't know," my husband answered, not realizing I was talking to myself. "We must be missing something." He stood suddenly. "Do we have any more money in the house?" he asked, looking at me expectantly.

I fished a clay pot from it's hiding place. As I turned it over on the table, two small coins fell out. "That's all we have left." He picked up one of the coins and looked at me. Then he snatched up the second coin and ran out the door toward the temple. He was going to give all that we had—what more could a god want?

*   *   *

"We must find water," the household governor told the king.

"Yes . . . yes, you are quite right," the king nodded.

"I will make a thorough search at once, your majesty." The governor bowed low as if to leave.

"Just a moment—not so fast. I am going with you. It is very important that we find water for our livestock, today." As the king rose to walk through the lofty halls of his palace, he waved his hand and his most trusted servant followed him. When they had made preparations, the governor and the king mounted horses and rode north to search for water, accompanied by the king's personal bodyguards.

Traveling through the wasted country, the king and his servant saw the bones of many animals—the hunter and the hunted alike had died of thirst and starvation. Many of the weathered bones were clearly livestock—their owners powerless to save them.

When they had traveled a fair distance from the palace, the king halted. "We must split up," he said bravely. " I will go this way and you that," he said, pointing west. The governor nodded gravely and turned his horse westward to search for brooks and streams that might still be flowing. The King's bodyguards split up as well—half going with the king and half with his servant.

The governor made a diligent and thorough search of several well-known sources of water, but they were dry. He dismounted and poured water from his water skin into his cupped hand. His horse thrust her muzzle into his hand and licked at the water. She was hot and tired and very thirsty.

"What are we going to do?" the governor asked the mare as he turned and led her back down the small hill. Looking out across the dusty land, he saw the figure of a man coming toward him. "Who could be way out here? Is it . . . oh my . . . could it be?"

The governor raced through thick dust to meet the lone figure. When the governor reached him, he threw his arms around the man. "Is it really you?"

"Yes." The man's black eyes sparkled.

"How did you get here? Where did you come from?"

"It's not important. We don't have time to waste."

"Well, what are you doing here?" The governor motioned for the bodyguards to back off.

"Go tell your king that I am here."

The king's servant shuddered. "What terrible thing have I done to deserve this? If I tell my king that you are here, he will be angry!" He moved closer to the man with the black eyes and spoke in a soft plea, "Sir, the king has been searching for you for three years. The Queen has also sent search parties after you. They have declared you to be the number-one *enemy of the state*. Diplomats from every surrounding nation have sworn that you are not within their borders." The governor fell to his knees. "Don't you understand that you are asking me to risk my own life to tell the king that you are here. And not only that, but the king will surely have you assassinated as well."

* * *

My husband returned home in the late morning, hungry and tired. "Let's go to the palace and demand the king to do something before we all die." Anger flooded his face.

After a meager meal we bundled our two hungry children against the merciless sun and dust storms and headed for the palace. We were surprised to find a throng had already gathered outside the palace. Everyone was in a bad temper and kept goading each other into shouting at the king.

Suddenly the queen emerged from inside the palace. She walked briskly toward us from the front door that was flung wide to allow her passage. Stopping at the top of the steps she held up her hands to command our silence.

When the mob was hushed she looked slowly around and then in an overly irritated tone she addressed those assembled at the front of her home.

"What is this?" she demanded. "What are all of you doing here?" She glared at us—all of us.

"We want rain!" a man from the crowd yelled, shattering the silence.

"We want the king to come out here and face us like a man!" shouted someone to our right.

"My children are starving before my very eyes," I heard myself shriek in anger and frustration.

"Your king is not here. He has gone out on a quest in your behalf. Go home and pray that you will be forgiven for distrusting your god and your king. I also suggest that you find the thing that is most important in your life—the thing that may be coming between you and god. Bring it to the temple to

show that you are loyal to god and maybe you will be blessed."
She seemed to spit the words at us in contempt. After giving
us a long, deadly stare, she turned on her heel and retreated
into the palace, leaving an army in her wake to disperse the
crowd.

We trudged home in even lower spirits. "How can we give
more than everything?" I shuddered, realizing the only things
we had left were ourselves and our children.

*   *   *

"Sire! Sire!" The king turned when he heard his governors
voice behind him.

"Did you find water?" The king's hope died as he saw his
servant's ashen face. "What is it?"

"Your majesty, I just came from . . ." The governor
hesitated.

"What is it?"

"Sire, the one who refuses to serve your god is here and he
wants to see you."

The king felt as if his heart would burst with anger and then
a cold white terror overtook him. A trembling began in his
stomach and continued out through his whole body until he
was shivering with anger and a strange foreboding. "What
. . . ," he stammered. "When . . . ," he tried again but couldn't
finish. "Where . . . ," the king was unable to speak another
word. The king's soldiers moved closer as if to comfort the one
whom they were sworn to protect.

The king nodded and the small company followed the
governor's leading. It didn't take them long to reach the place
where the prophet waited. He was seated on a stone but stood
when the king dismounted his horse.

The two men stood face to face.

"Is it you?" the king demanded.   The prophet didn't respond. "You are the reason that god is mad at my whole nation. Just look at the land and the desolation you have caused."

"I have not brought this trouble on you," the prophet said without flinching.   "You are the one who has brought this trouble upon yourself and your nation. You and your father before you turned away from the living God. You have thrown away the true understanding of God and have believed lies." The prophet's voice was clear and his words of truth seemed to stun the king who stood before him unable to move.

"Look," the prophet commanded, pointing northwest.

"What?" The king looked where the prophet was pointing.

"See that mountain peak?" The king nodded. "Gather the people of your nation there and I will meet with them," the prophet continued in a commanding voice. "You come as well, along with all of your religious leaders."

The king turned at once to his bodyguards and pointed out three of them. "You . . . you . . . and you, return to the palace and see that it is made so."

The three guards turned quickly and returned through the dust to the palace.

*   *   *

"Did you hear that?" my husband rolled over on his cot.

"What was it?" I sat upright, worry making my heart race. It was dark outside and we had been asleep when the sound of voices roused us. My husband stumbled out the doorway to find the neighbors muttering over an announcement they had heard.

"What's going on?" he asked.

"We have been summoned by the king," one neighbor complained.

40

"And that's not the worst of it," another neighbor chimed in. "No," the first neighbor picked up his story again, "you know that man we've been hearing about—the man who is supposed to be a prophet?" When my husband didn't answer the neighbor continued, "You know, that guy whose the number-one enemy of the state?"

"Oh, him," my husband finally responded.

"Yes, well, we are supposed to meet him and the king on some mountain."

"Uh-huh, and we are supposed to leave at first light."

I scrambled back from the doorway where I had been listening. "What was that all about?" I asked as my husband shuffled back inside.

"We must leave on a little trip at first light. We have been summoned by the king and the prophet."

"You mean that bad guy everyone's talking about?" My voice sounded hoarse even to my own ears. My husband simply nodded.

"It's almost dawn now." I looked out of the open doorway. My heart was pounding. I looked at my husband. He just sat on his cot and shook his head. After a moment he grunted and shook his head some more.

"Well, don't just sit there, help me." I finally said, wondering if he was all right.

He got up and began packing for the trip while I found a few bread crusts and dried fruit for our breakfast. When we were packed and had eaten, we joined our neighbors who were trudging to the northwest. Everyone talked among themselves in whispers.

"I don't like this whole business . . . marching for days on end through the dust and then ending up on a desolate mountain top," one man said.

"Why should we do what the prophet says? It's his fault

we're all starving!" another man said. There were many grunts
of agreement and nods from the men.

"Some new disaster is about to happen, I can feel it in my
bones," an old woman said, shuffling along with her walking
stick. Then it was the women's turn to nod in agreement and
exclaim that there was a strangeness to the air around them.

"Why are we going to the mountain?" every child seemed
to be asking. We could only shake our heads in dismay and
wonder.

*   *   *

The dark sky seemed strange and unnatural to those of us
encamped on the slopes of the mountain. Our curiosity and
dread had grown with each step during the many days it had
taken us to reach our destination.   There was an uneasiness
in the air and everyone was nervous. Most of the men were
sitting in the flaps of their tents staring out into the darkness,
wondering what terrible calamity would be called down on our
nation.

None of us noticed the lone figure making his way toward
the top of the mountain. None of us noticed as he slipped
around boulders and stepped carefully through the darkness.
We didn't hear him when he knelt in prayer to pour out his
heart to God. We didn't see the tears that fell from the eyes of
one whose heart was breaking for all of us.

We just sat silently in our tents hating him and the God we
didn't know. We sat in the dark not realizing the blindness of
our deceived hearts; not knowing that we had drifted away from
our God step by step until we didn't know who sent the dew
and rain to water our land. We didn't know that up on the
mountain a man prayed for us.

"God open their eyes," he prayed, in his solitude. "They
are so blind; help them to see the truth. Show them beyond all

doubt that you alone are God. Win their hearts back to You."
He prayed from the depths of his heart with tears steaming
down his weathered face. *"I am only one little man who is in
constant need of You. Hold my heart, Lord; keep me firmly
where you have placed me. I pray that I won't get in your way."*

At dawn the tension thickened. The king, his body guards,
the religious leaders and the general masses of our nation all
assembled at the mountain. Thousands of us swarmed up the
mountain sides from the lower valleys all the way to the
summit.

My husband and I arrived at the top, out of breath from
carrying our children. I stood panting as I looked at the huge
throng about me. We had all answered the call to assemble on
this mountain—though we still did not know why.

I looked anxiously around trying to see the prophet whose
command had summoned us to such a strange place. Then I
saw him and I couldn't keep myself from staring curiously at
him—it was the same man I had seen walking in the desert. I
did not see the tear stains or the broken heart. Instead, I saw
a man standing in front of us without fear or worry. His face
was calm yet very solemn. I couldn't believe that he looked so
peaceful standing before a whole nation who hated him with
such passion. Yet when I looked at his face, it seemed as if we
were the ones who were standing before him and I trembled.

Then the prophet raised his arms and the thronging
masses were quieted. He cupped his hands to his mouth and
called out in a clear trumpet-like voice, "When will you stop
listening to the mere opinions of others?" His words spilled
down over the mountain in clear tones as we listened intently.

"If the Creator is truly God, then follow him," he called, his
voice echoing like music. "But if the god of your own creation
is worthy, then follow him."

43

As the echoing words died away, total silence blanketed the mountain and for a moment I had to ponder what he meant by those words. Then a curious feeling began to stir in my heart. Watching breathlessly, it seemed as if the prophet was waiting for someone to respond. I wondered at the feelings inside of me. My heart was flooded with a longing to believe that the choice was that simple. *Could I just choose?* Soon, the silence became uncomfortable and men started shuffling about, clearing their throats. Still the prophet waited. I wondered if anyone would dare to stand with him. I wondered if anyone would risk his life to stand for the Creator. I took a deep breath. I could picture myself moving forward to stand by the prophet but when I exhaled, doubt filled my thoughts and hatred of the man gripped my heart when he called out again.

"I stand before you, one man—as a representative of the Living God, to challenge you and the god of your making."

The mountain buzzed with excitement.

"He's signing his own death warrant," one man whispered.

"He's crazy!" someone else said.

The prophet held up his hands and the crowds slowly quieted. "I propose that we set up two altars. One for your god and one for my God. We will place a sacrifice on each altar. Then we will pray, and the god that answers by fire is the true God."

Another murmur ran instantly through the throngs of people. Many nodded to each other and blinked at the logic of the simple proposal. The prophet's plan was so reasonable that our leaders had to comply.

"Yes, it is a good idea!" someone had the courage to answer.

"Well spoken," another yelled out.

"Yes," many agreed, but I wasn't one of them. My heart was still gripped in a fierce lock of hatred. The prophet had no idea what we had lived through. He didn't know us. We hardly knew him, except for one thing—we knew that it was because of him that we were all starving to death.

I turned to look at our nation's religious leaders. They were huddled together and I moved through the crowd to hear what they were saying. I wanted to be assured that the crazy prophet would pay for what he had caused us to suffer.

"There's no way out of this," one leader whispered.

"We'll figure something out," an elderly leader answered. "Now put on your faces."

My heart sank. What was happening? It seemed a horrible nightmare. Were the leaders really so unsure of themselves. Were they unsure of what they had taught us? I peered at their faces but they looked unafraid and proud. I watched closely as they prepared the wood and the sacrifice and laid it on the altar. I listened intently as they began to chant their spells that I had heard a thousand times before.

"Hear us, O hear us. We are your faithful servants," they sang as they gathered around the altar. They bowed then knelt and prayed . . . they got up again and sang songs . . . and then started all over again. Soon they began to chant their prayers and sing much louder until they were screaming. Many of the people even came forward to show their devotion to the god being summoned. Then I noticed that the leaders were panting and beginning to tear out their hair. I had never seen them do that before, though it did make them appear to be very devoted. After a couple of hours their chants seemed strangled and their screaming seemed to be full of agony.

I watched and waited all morning but god did not send the fire. The leaders seemed to grow more and more frantic. They began to hit themselves and each other. After a while they performed a ceremony that seemed altogether uncalled for and I slumped to the ground sick.

Feeling dizzy I lay in the dust with my eyes shut, listening. I could hear the chants echoing all around the mountain. Those around me were pressing closer to watch as the ceremonies became more and more captivating.

"Light it," I heard one prophet whisper to another.

"I can't," he answered back through clenched teeth.

"Why not?"

"The prophet is watching me."

"Well, he can't watch you all the time, just wait until you have the chance."

I wretched. Feeling utterly hopeless I crawled back to my husband who stooped when he saw me. "Are you all right?" he asked, looking concerned. I nodded and he helped me stand.

"The children shouldn't be watching this awful display."

"No, let them watch," he answered firmly. I was too weak to argue with him, but couldn't help holding their tiny little hands in mine.

"Mommy, why are those men bleeding?" my daughter asked. Her large eyes looking up at me with concern.

I stifled a sob and bent to talk to her.

"They are cutting themselves," I said with tears in my eyes.

"Why?" she asked.

"They are trying to make god happy."

"Does blood make god happy?" She starting to cry.

"I don't know, honey," I blubbered. "Sh-h, here let Mommy hold you." I picked her up in my arms. It was comforting to hold her but she soon squirmed to watch the leaders at the altar and I had to put her down. We watched the rest of the morning together, but there was no fire.

At noon we heard the prophet's voice calling out. He seemed to be making fun of our religious leaders. I knew I should be offended, but I was too sickened by the ceremonies to care any more.

I was shocked to hear my husband snicker at the prophet's comments. He quickly stopped when I jabbed his ribs with my elbow. His face turned red and he held up his hands but he didn't say anything. I shook my head at him and looked at our children. They were staring wide eyed at the disgusting spectacle before us.

"Look, they are trying to divert the prophet's attention," my husband whispered in my ear. I looked closer. It did seem like a couple of them were trying to hide something in their hands.

"Do you think they are trying to light the fire?" I whispered.

My husband nodded. "It seems obvious enough to me that they aren't going to get any answer to their pleas, but if they succeed in lighting that altar, this crowd will tear the prophet to pieces." I nodded, comprehending how strong our hatred for the prophet had grown week by week as the drought had worsened.

When the prophet had first appeared in the king's court three years before, it had all seemed a silly jest. He had told the king that it wouldn't rain until he—the prophet—said it would. I remember how we had all laughed. We believed the sun, rain, dew and even storms were sent because of our goodness. We knew that we were being blessed because of our hard work.

My husband had been a cattle rancher before the drought had reduced him to a part-time handy man. That was a blow to him and it made me wonder how he could have any pity for the prophet, yet there wasn't any fire on our leaders' altar.

I looked at my husband who looked back at me with a strange look that bordered on tenderness. I looked quickly away, afraid I might cry. I felt so hot and weak. The leaders were going on and on and things were getting worse and worse by the minute. They looked worn out and confused and they

47

were weak from loss of blood. I couldn't understand why they didn't just give up. Then I stopped myself and wondered at my own feelings. Only a few hours before I, too, was praying for fire.

I looked back at the leaders who were all huddled together. They seemed to be having a debate among themselves. After a short time one of them approached the prophet and sneered at him. Then he turned toward the crowd and said, "Our god is angry because of this man," he pointed at the prophet. "Our god will not stoop to answer us as long as he is alive."

"Let him try!" My husband shouted.

"Yeah, give him a chance," someone agreed. The leader stood defiantly and held up his hands. "Even though our god will not stoop to answer we are generous men and will allow this man his opportunity," he said. Then in a voice full of contempt he addressed the prophet, "It's your turn, Elijah." Then he turned and walked quickly back to stand with the other leaders to watch.

Elijah walked forward from where he had been standing. I held my breath. The whole mountain seemed to be holding it's breath with me in anticipation of what would happen next. After a long moment of silence, the prophet's voice rang out over the top of the mountain. "Come near to me," he called, in a gracious voice full of tender pity. I noticed that he seemed almost choked by tears of emotion. Fearfully we moved closer to him and watched as he knelt by the old broken-down altar of his God to repair it. I could see that it was precious to him, though it was only a pile of rubble.

Stone by stone he lovingly repaired the altar. I couldn't help noticing the difference between the chaotic ceremonies of the leaders and the calm presence of Elijah.

When he had repaired the altar, he dug a trench around it, and laid wood on it. Then, after placing the sacrifice on top of the wood, the prophet called for four barrels of water. My husband and many others were quick to respond. They poured the four large barrels of water over the sacrifice, soaking it. The prophet walked all the way around the altar and then called out, "Do it again." After inspecting it the second time, he called out, "Do it once again."

I watched as the men were pouring the last of the twelve barrels over the altar. There was so much water that it filled the trench and ran out over the parched earth. The prophet nodded, then turned and walked right up to us. Many of us trembled in fear, but he looked lovingly at us with so much compassion and he spoke in such kind words that I soon forgot my fears.

"The Creator-God loves you." Elijah then pointed in my direction and our eyes met. "He loves all of us," he said, smiling. My heart leapt.

As I watched the prophet turned and his smile faded. When he began to talk again he looked and sounded deadly serious. "What you believe about God is life or death to you. The truth about who he is and what he is like is the difference between life or death. You don't leave important choices about your well being in the hands of others . . . why do you stake your eternal lives on the idle opinions of those around you? Search for the truth. Find out who God is for yourselves. "Please, . . . let God into your hearts and minds. He will show himself to you if you will let him." The prophet paused, his voice showering down the mountain.

Then as if in answer to our silent questions he said, "You work very hard at being righteous people, but God does not ask you to make yourselves into his faithful people. He is the one who does the making, the creating." Elijah took another step forward. "Please, . . . humble your hearts and turn back to the God of your fathers before it is too late. Turn back to him and he will remove the drought from this land." The prophet's words and tone of voice brought tears to many eyes in the crowd as he continued to plead with us to find the truth. "I know it is difficult," he said, nodding his head. "I know that troubles weigh heavily on your weary hearts, but God can heal your hearts and your land, if you will only let him. Let him prove that he is a God worthy of your trust and adoration . . . please . . . please." The prophet couldn't seem to speak any more. It was as if he was choked by an overwhelming desire to weep for the people he loved so much. He turned and walked to the ancient altar.

Once again profound silence dominated the slopes of the mountain. Elijah bowed his head before the assembly and I wondered if that was all he was going to do. I wondered why he didn't move around and chant and scream. I looked at his face and saw that he was at peace and for the first time in my life I thought that maybe God was really different than I had thought.

Then he prayed. *"Lord God of Abraham, Isaac, and of Israel, let it be known this day that you are God in Israel and that I am your servant, and that I have done all these things at Your word. Hear me O Lord, hear me, that this people may know that you are the Lord God, and that you have turned their hearts back to you."*

Barely had he finished his prayer when God answered. The whole mountain was suddenly lit up. Our eyes were dazzled by the brilliant flames and flashes of fire descending from heaven. We threw ourselves down to the ground in awe, afraid to look at the fire.

"God is going to burn me up for not worshiping him," I whimpered in terror.

When the fire was spent we slowly got to our feet. Smoke and ashes were all that remained of the mighty answer from

Heaven. The fire had not only consumed the sacrifice, but the altar of stones and all the water in the trench.

I thought my heart was going to leap right out of my chest when all of us cried out together, in one voice, "The Creator, he is God; the Creator, he is God!"

I looked at my husband. "I can see that the Creator is God but I don't understand what happened. I mean the two altars looked the same.

My husband nodded. "Yes, they looked almost the same. They were both made of stone and they both had wood and a sacrifice on them."

"So how were they different?"

He looked kindly at me and then said, "The difference was in the hearts of the worshipers."

"How do you know what was in their hearts?"

"By watching them. Our religious leaders were doing everything they could to get their angry god to answer them. You saw them. They chanted and screamed . . ."

"Oh, yes . . . it was horrendous. They did everything they could to get fire to appear. They danced and waved their arms and even cut themselves."

"Yes . . . they even gave of their own life's blood to please their god."

"But it didn't work!"

"No, it didn't."

"But they did so much. They thought they were worshiping the life giver."

"It doesn't matter how hard you work to please God. You can't—we can't."

"What are you saying?"

"I'm saying that we can work and give of ourselves until it kills us and we still can't please God."

"I don't understand."

"It's what the prophet said. He asked us to turn back to God and let him heal us. That has to be what pleases God."

"So . . . you're saying that if we don't let God change us there's nothing we can do to please him even if we are doing all of the right things?"

He nodded. "Even if we are working really hard at all the right things?" He nodded again.

"That's seems backwards."

He nodded, tears brimming in his eyes. "I know," he choked. "We were taught to work hard to get God's attention, but God was trying to get ours. We were just too busy doing all of the right things to see it." My husband held me close and sobbed into my shoulder.

I wondered if I would ever understand. It all seemed so confusing. I stood looking over my husbands shoulder. I had a good view of the prophet's face. As I looked at him I could see that he was watching us with wonder in his eyes. He saw a whole nation being set free from deception. It was as if God's fire was burning right through the darkness of our hearts and opening our eyes to see the truth.

I suddenly realized that I had been trying to please god with my own goodness. I had been doing everything I believed was right and good. I had believed what others had told me instead of seeking for truth—I had worked so hard but had been so lazy!

"So, if we come to God in our own goodness then there will be no fire." Suddenly I understood.

"That's what I am beginning to understand," my husband nodded.

"We needed God's fire from Heaven to be able to see that when we come to God, knowing our weakness . . . understanding our need of him . . . then . . . then . . .God will answer with fire!"

Again, my husband nodded.

We left the mountain as a family and a nation. All of us trudging toward home chattering togther, not even complaining about the choking dust, when all of a sudden we stopped. No one said a word. We looked at each other with surprise and joy as something wonderful was happening . . . *it was raining!*

Fire from Heaven

It was a cool morning when I slipped quietly from my bed and dressed. I wanted to go to the office early so I could get some work done before I attended a planning meeting at the temple for the annual festival.

"Where are you going so early?"

"To the office."

"It's not even daybreak."

"I know," I said, kissing my wife on the forehead.

"You work too hard," she sighed and rolled over.

She was always telling me that. I knew she didn't understand my fear of not gaining God's approval and I didn't explain it to her. I just continued to drive myself to be the best man I could. I hoped that one day, she would understand.

Finishing my work early I walked to the temple. When I arrived I saw that someone had marked the courtyard with chalk to divide the perimeter into small sections which I guessed were booths. There were always new vendors seeking booth space to sell their wares at the festival.

I walked slowly around the quiet courtyard and tried to imagine the throngs of people who would soon arrive in the city. Everyone would come to the temple to offer a sacrifice to God in order to obtain his favor and blessing for another year. Most would come with a heart searching for forgiveness and inner peace.

I wondered if they would find it here or if they would return home from their yearly pilgrimage unchanged. I also wondered if it would be easier this year for the poor than it had been in the past. I had grown tired of the high prices they were forced to pay from their empty pockets. They were always filled with fear because without a sacrifice they couldn't be forgiven and accepted by God. I was thankful that I was not a poor man.

I shook the thought from my head and walked quickly toward the meeting room. I had lost track of time and now I was late.

"How are plans going for the annual event?" the chairman asked as I took my seat.

"Things are going well. We were able to squeeze in several extra booths this year for more merchants," one of my associates explained excitedly. Every one nodded their head and smiled at the prospect of the extra revenue.

The meeting was short and when I arrived home early my wife was pleasantly surprised.

"What are you doing home so early? Is everything all right?" she asked with concern.

I smiled at her. "I just wanted to help you with dinner."

She smiled back and put me to work setting the table.

"How was your day?" She asked sounding happy.

"It was good until I went to a meeting at the temple. Would you believe they are going to have twelve extra booths this year during the festival?"

"Twelve?"

"Yes . . . can you believe it?"

"You don't sound very happy about it."

"Well, I'm not completely comfortable with selling things in the temple courtyard."

"I thought you were helping the people by providing a service for those who couldn't bring their own sacrifice."

"I used to think it was a service until I saw how much the merchants were charging everyone."

"Oh?"

"Yes, it seems we have created an opportunity for the merchants to steal from people by overcharging them."

During the next few days even though I was very busy preparing for the thousands of visitors coming to town, I began to feel restless and I just wanted the whole thing to be over. As the festivities were getting underway I decided to go home to get away from the crowds. But on my way I made a quick stop by the temple to see how things were going.

Merchants were packed next to each other around the perimeter of the courtyard and the noise was unbearable. Customers bartered and argued with the merchants. The poor people begged and cried. The vendors shouted and demanded the highest prices while they shoved coins into their pockets. Caged animals added to the noise and stench.

I was sickened by what I saw. A poor family tried to purchase a dove. "We don't have enough money," the man whispered to the merchant.

"Well, then I guess you won't be forgiven of your sins and God will curse you," the merchant sneered.

I could feel my blood pressure rising—it had never bothered me much in the past. I was sure though that it wasn't right to put a price on God's love and forgiveness. I realized I paid a price every day to earn it but somehow it didn't seem the same.

The poor man's young wife began to cry. "We've come so far," she pleaded.

The merchant just shrugged and called, "Next."

The couple walked sorrowfully away and the merchant turned to the vendor in the next booth. "They'll come up with the money some how," he said.

I was disgusted . . . it wasn't right to deny others of our nation the privilege to participate in the Passover celebration.

I stood in the bustling crowd of worshipers wondering if God could possibly be in the midst of all the chaos when suddenly everyone became quiet. I looked around and didn't see anything out of the ordinary but the silence was so heavy. I turned to see what had caused the sudden hush and then I saw him---a man stood just inside the entry way. He looked around at everyone and they shrank away from him.

Unable to take my eyes from him, I watched as those near me hid their faces and fled from his gaze. He slowly descended the steps toward the merchants' booths as they jumped up with cries of terror and scrambled out the gates.

When the man reached the bottom step he tipped over one of the tables and spilled the money on the floor. The clinking of the coins echoed throughout the courtyard.

"Take these things out of here," he said. "Don't make a mockery out of my Father's house . . . his gifts are free."

The few remaining merchants fled in terror. Many of the worshipers made a rush for the gates, too. It seemed that almost everyone ran for their lives. I realized that I was trembling, too, but I slipped behind a pillar to watch what would happen next. Some others remained as well. I stayed for a long time, unable to tear myself from the scene.

As I watched a new thought began to take shape in my mind. There were clearly two groups of people. It reminded me of Cain and Abel. They, too, were both professed worshipers of God, yet only one received fire from heaven.

I had always pondered the difference between the two and now I felt that this man knew the answer.

When I finally left the temple my heart was racing and I couldn't wait to get home to tell my wife what I had seen and heard.

"Oh Nick, that is incredible," she said when I told her about the man in the courtyard.

"What happened after all the merchants ran out?"

"Oh, Darling . . . you would have loved it. The poor and the sick people gathered around the man and the children sang and took turns sitting in his lap."

"Wow . . . that's amazing."

"It was one of the most wonderful things I have ever seen. And that's not all . . . he didn't just talk to everyone . . . he told them that their sins were freely forgiven."

"He did that after they had sacrificed their offerings to God, right?"

"No . . . well some of the people had . . . but most of them hadn't, I'm sure.

"What? How could he say that if they hadn't performed a sacrifice yet? Is he a priest?"

"I'm not sure, but you know what I think?"

"What?"

"I think he might be a prophet sent here by God to clean up the temple."

"What do you mean?"

"Well . . . you know . . . all those merchants charging the poor people too much for animals to sacrifice. When they can't buy one to perform the ceremony it fills them with fear because they think they will be cursed and abandoned by God."

"And you said . . . the man . . . what's his name?"

"Jesus."

"Jesus was telling people they were forgiven without their sacrifices?"

"Yes. He said, 'God's gifts are free.' Then he healed all the sick people."

"He healed them? What do you mean?"

"I mean, he made the sick people well—really and truly well."

"Are you sure?"

"Yes . . . I saw it with my own eyes."

"Who is he, Nick?"

"I'm not sure but I'm going to find out."

That night while everyone was sleeping I went to look for Jesus. I found him in a secluded place and asked for a meeting with him and he agreed.

"Thank you for meeting with me," I said trying to hide how nervous I was. "I can tell that you are a man of God, otherwise you wouldn't have been able to heal all of those people today." I felt small and timid next to this man even though he was very plain and simple.

"If you want to go to heaven you need to be reborn," he said, ignoring the compliment I had just given him.

"What? Are you saying that I'm not qualified for heaven the way I am?" I was stunned. I had always followed every rule and fulfilled every duty that was expected of a man of my position. "How can a grown man be born again?" I asked sarcastically. His answer puzzled me.

"Unless your heart is cleansed and remade by the Spirit of God, you cannot go to Heaven.

"Why?"

"You have learned all of the rules but have those rules changed your life? Have they given you peace?"

"No . . ."

"Have those rules helped you become a better person?"

"No, I wouldn't say that but those rules have given me a guideline to work toward."

"Rules can point us in a direction but they cannot make us go there. For example, if you had a rule about always drinking clean water in the morning and one of your servants poured you a glass of dirty water, what would that mean?"

"Well, it would mean that the water had gotten dirty somewhere between the well and me."

"Yes and if you then discovered that the water pitcher was where the dirt came from what would you do?"

"I would have the pitcher washed thoroughly, of course."

"Did your rule about clean drinking water make the pitcher clean?"

"No . . . the washing did."

"That's what you need . . . to be washed clean on the

inside. No matter how much clean water you pour into the jar it will always pour out dirty until the jar is clean."

"Does that mean that without my heart being washed clean I can't do anything good? Because if that's so, then I can't keep God's law until I am changed. Is that what you are saying?

"Yes . . . you need a new heart."

"But I have kept every rule. I have sacrificed the purest of lambs. I have contributed large sums of my time and money to the temple and my community. Don't those count for anything?"

"Unless the heart is pure it cannot keep the law. The law is a description of what a man will be like when he is pure from the inside out. A pure heart will generate pure and holy thoughts and actions."

I had never heard such things before and my mind was whirling. Was it true that I had worked so hard to be perfect and it wasn't enough? Could it be possible that Heaven truly was a place that was too pure for me?

"Are you saying that my heart isn't purified by what I do?"

"That's exactly right. A godly life is not a mere change of habits, but rather a total transformation . . . a cleansing of the inner character. Everyone who wants to see Heaven must go through this change and it is only possible through the Spirit of God."

We talked late into the night and I found myself wanting not only to know more, but to experience the change that Jesus was describing to me. I wanted to be a better person. I wanted to be more like God.

*   *   *

Footsteps echoed through the stone halls of the secret meeting place. A small, plushly decorated room quickly filled with somber faced men.

60

"Who does he think he is anyway?" a voice full of anger asked. It was the voice of the most powerful man in Israel. Dressed in beautiful robes of linen the high priest almost spat out his words.

"He thinks he is the son of God or something," a younger priest answered.

"Did he actually say that?" a finely dressed man asked.

"He called the temple his father's house," a fourth man chimed in as he stepped into the room from the hallway.

"That's blasphemy," an old man said tugging at his beard.

"What shall we do? He's bound to start another movement like the one that baptizer, John, started," the high priest said, still seething with anger.

"I hate movements . . . I say we squash it," the old man said, standing.

"Yeah . . . let's not let another movement sweep our nation. Every time the people get excited about someone they become disrespectful toward our high and holy office as spiritual leaders," the high priest added.

"Every time there is a new independent leader we are always made out to be the bad guys. Let's put a stop to this now," the youngest priest said.

"Okay, but there's something I want to know first," the high priest said, looking around the room at his associates. "Why did you all run away today when Jesus walked into the temple?"

There was a long moment of silence before someone finally spoke up. "It was eerie . . . I felt like he was looking straight into me," the old man said.

"I felt like he was reading my mind and that he knew everything about me . . . even things my wife doesn't know," another said.

"That's exactly how I felt," the youngest of the group gasped, nodding his head.

"I couldn't get out fast enough," the high priest agreed. "Let's squash this thing before it's too late. Let's send some spies out and see what they can dig up."

*   *   *

After the night that Jesus and I talked privately, I couldn't seem to forget the things that he told me. I read the scrolls to discover whether or not what he said agreed with the ancient prophets.

It seemed the more time I spent reading the scrolls, the more I began to see things in my life that were not pure and holy and I was humbled.

What if Jesus was right? Maybe heaven is too pure for me. I vowed to try harder. I would be good at my job. I would be the ultimate husband. I would continue to be a role model in my community even if I had to work at it constantly.

*   *   *

"Our spies have brought back news," the high priest addressed his fellow priests.

"What did they say?" everyone wanted to know.

"They said that the movement is very dangerous, but they aren't really sure how to stop it without assassinating the leader."

"Will that work or will that just make him a martyr?" someone else wanted to know.

"We need to have an analysis done. Let's have those figures worked out so we can determine what would be better. By the way . . . keep your heads up . . . we believe the Pharisees have infiltrated the group," the high priest said with a scowl.

*   *   *

Spending time in my office one day, I came across a memo stating that Jesus was to be pursued and found guilty of breaking the law. The date on the memo was several weeks old. I wondered why I hadn't noticed it before and then realized that it wasn't written to me, but rather to one of my associates. Possibly he was trying to let me know what was going on without getting himself in trouble. I quickly cleaned off my desk, locked my door and headed for home.

"I'm out of the loop," I told my wife as I entered the door.
"What do you mean?"

"Look at this memo."

"Oh, Nick, this doesn't sound good."

"No it doesn't."

"What are you going to do?"

"There is a meeting scheduled for this evening and I plan to attend. I want to do whatever I can to stop this campaign against Jesus—he is a godly man."

"Be careful," my wife pleaded.

* * *

"I want to start this meeting off with an update from those on the inside of the movement," the chairman said addressing the assembly. A man stood and cleared his throat. He was the one assigned to keep tabs on those who had infiltrated the group commonly known as "the followers of Jesus."

"Our people have successfully joined the group but have been unable to find anything to use against the leader. They are quiet certain that they could find plenty against many of the group members, though."

"Well, lets just keep them in place. They are bound to come across something sooner or later," the chairman said.

After the meeting was over I walked out to a garden and sat down. Looking up at the evening sky I wondered how far my associates would go in tracking down the core beliefs of the movement they were so concerned about. Would they discover that Jesus was as peace loving and truthful as I had observed when I secretly met with him.

"What are you doing, Nick?" the chairman asked as he joined me in the garden.

"Just wondering how things will turn out," I responded.

"That depends on where this thing is leading."

I nodded and looked at my friend's weathered face. "It may be a good thing," I said.

"It may be, but from what I've seen it is seductive and dangerous and the leader is very popular."

"What do you mean, dangerous?"

"Well, the leader promotes freedom."

"Isn't that what we all want?"

"Yes, but not the kind of freedom he promotes."

"What is he promoting?"

"Love, peace and harmony. He promises freedom from sin if we will turn toward God but he is missing one important element."

"What's that?"

"He's leaving out the part about what we have to do to attain this freedom. It isn't just something you accept. It's something you have to work very hard for."

"But what if he was sent to help us see our errors. What if he is giving us some long over-due warnings? You know as well as I do that our pattern has been to ignore and then kill those who have come to help us. That's why we are so oppressed by our Roman rulers."

"Yes, you are right, Nick. It cannot be denied that our history is stained with the blood of innocent men. However, we will not repeat the mistakes of our ancestors. We have everything under control . . . we are doing everything right. We are even going beyond the call of duty.

"What do you mean?"

"Over the years we have added new laws of our own to help the people obey God's law. When the Messiah comes to deliver us he will see that we are still God's special people and he will free us from the Roman bondage. Everything is in place . . . now it's just a matter of keeping the people in line while we wait. That's why we cannot allow anyone to get us off track."

* * *

"How has our analysis turned out?" The high priest leaned forward in anticipation.

"We cannot be sure, but we believe it would be better to eliminate the leader and disband the group, even if we create a martyr," one of the priests answered.

"I agree," the oldest priest said, pounding his fist on the shiny table.

"We must come up with a fool-proof plan and quickly," the high priest said with a deadly gleam in his eyes.

* * *

"Things are heating up around the nation," I told my wife. "How are you holding up?"

"I'm troubled, but I'm ok."

"What troubles you, may I ask?"

"You can ask me anything—you know that."

I told her about the conversation I had with my superior earlier in the day. I shared my feelings and concerns about what the future held for us. She listened quietly and nodded her head.

"I share your concerns . . . so what is the bottom line?" she asked with her usual perception.

"To be honest with you I think the main issue is power. No

one wants a newcomer to become so popular with the common people. Whoever has the most influence has the most power."

"I see what you mean, but what about your associates' sense of right and wrong? What about their great piety."

"It's all distorted. No one is really who they seem to be and my mind is sort of muddled . . . I'm not sure what or who to believe anymore."

*　　*　　*

"How did the meeting with the Pharisees go?" the oldest priest asked looking around the meeting room at the others.

"They are willing to make this a joint effort," the high priest answered.

"Finally . . . something we can agree on," the old man smiled.

"We have found someone on the inside who is willing to help us," the high priest said, smiling back at the old man.

"Good work. What are they willing to do for us?"

"Give us information and provide us with an opportunity to bring this whole thing to an end, very quietly."

"Excellent. How much will it cost us?"

"A mere pittance."

*　　*　　*

"We had a meeting this morning," one of my fellow Pharisees whispered.

"Why wasn't I notified?" I asked looking up quickly.

"Because they are tired of your cautious advice and they are worried about you. They aren't sure about your loyalties."

"That doesn't sound good," I said, my stomach in knots. My associate shook his head and disappeared out of my office. I sat back in my chair then quickly made up my mind. I grabbed my things and headed for home.

"The inside man is ready," the high priest whispered.

"Now?" the old man asked?

"Yes. We are to do it tonight."

"Are we ready?"

"Does it matter?"

"No, we must move quickly."

* * *

"He did it again," I said breathlessly, bursting through the front door.

"Who did what?" my wife asked, hurrying over to me.

"Jesus . . . he sent the merchants running out of the temple again just like he did three years ago."

"Really? What happened?"

"The same thing."

"They're going to kill him aren't they?" her face was full of fear and sorrow.

"Don't jump to conclusions."

"I'm not jumping to conclusions . . . I'm basing them on the things you have told me."

"Well, I know every one's doing a lot of talking but they are still godly men. Surely they won't go that far."

I was almost ready to go to bed when I heard a commotion outside my door. One of my associates stepped into my home breathing hard.

"They've arrested him," he said between gasps.

"When?"

"A few hours ago."

"In the middle of the night?"

"They're trying to keep it quiet."

I heard my wife gasp. I turned to her and she held out my

coat. "Go," she nodded.

By the time we caught up with the crowd I could see that things were out of hand. People were screaming threats against a man that stood in the middle of the fray. I was pushed and jostled by the angry people around me and I was sickened by what I saw.

A man was standing there pale and bloodied and all around him was a seething mob of hate. The local governor was trying to silence the crowd. "What shall I do with him?" he asked.

"Let him be crucified," people everywhere yelled.

"What has he done to deserve death? I haven't found anything wrong with him. Let me punish him and let him go."

I watched the battered man's face. He was calm and serene. There was no hate or revenge on his face. Only quiet dignity. Suddenly I realized the man was indeed, Jesus. The realization hit me in the stomach and I doubled over. How could this happen?

I had seen the jealousy of the priests and rulers of my beloved nation but the depth of their malice toward Jesus was stunning.

Looking around me I saw that most of my associates were there. They had joined together with our sworn enemies, the Sadducees, to make this happen. It was sickening and I was afraid for my own life.

" Nick . . . Nick . . . Nicodemus!" my superior called me to join the group. I made my way through the crowd.

"Isn't this great?"

I looked into my friend's eyes and saw something that I had never seen before and I was truly terrified.

"Let him by crucified!" the mob screamed again. Everyone around me was raising their fists and chanting the death sentence. My associates were looking at me and chanting. I knew they expected me to join them in their wretched

From a distance I followed the group all morning and we ended up at Calvary. While there, hiding among the crowd, I watched as Jesus was nailed to a wooden cross. I witnessed the hatred and feelings of triumph that my closest friends and associates displayed. They were delirious with spite. Then I saw their delirium turn to terror when darkness hid the cross from our view and I heard their screams when lightning split the sky. I heard the tortured man on the cross forgive them and I wondered at his unselfishness.

Many strange thoughts seemed to whirl in my mind as the afternoon wore on. I continued to watch and listen. I felt like every word that Jesus spoke was somehow of vital importance so I stayed near him.

When all was quiet Jesus gave one final cry that sounded triumphant. Then he died.

"Truly this was the Son of God," I heard a Roman soldier say. A commotion erupted at the foot of Jesus' cross. Everyone seemed to be wondering if he was truly dead. The Pharisees and Sadducees were united in demanding that someone prove to them that Jesus was dead. A soldier standing near the cross thrust his spear into the dead man's side. I gasped aloud when blood and water flowed from the new wound.

Yes, he was dead and the cause of his quick death was a broken heart. I was deeply moved when I realized that he had not died from his wounds . . . he had not died from loss of blood . . . he had died from a heart that was crushed. And no wonder . . . I heard his tortured cry, "Father why have you forsaken me?" He was abandoned by God—something I had always feared. That's why I worked so hard.

It was then I realized that I was weeping and I slunk away feeling utterly wretched for offering him no assistance. I could have stood up for him. I could have at least voiced my opinion. Now, it seemed that all was lost and I was ashamed of myself.

Why hadn't I seen my own selfishness before now?

I returned home and sat weeping on my porch. "I'm wretched," I sobbed. "I killed him."

"What? How could you have?" my wife asked, walking toward me.

"I killed him by being more worried about myself than about what happened to the son of God."

She sat beside me and held my hand in hers.

"Why did they kill him? Didn't they know who he was?" she asked sadly.

"Yes, many of them knew, but they rejected him."

"Oh Nick, how could they?"

"They were disappointed in what he came to do."

"Why did he come?"

"He came to rescue us."

"From the Romans?"

"No. He came to rescue us from sin . . . from being completely cut off from God. He came to win us back to God by showing us the unconditional love and forgiveness of his Father.

"But I thought we worshiped and obeyed him so he would save us. We go to the altar and offer a sacrifice to God so he will forgive and accept us."

"I know that's what we have always been taught but we have misunderstood. We thought that God needed a sacrifice from us in order to want to save us. But Jesus said "If you have seen me you have seen the Father." Oh, Darling, you should have seen him. No matter how they treated him he was kind and forgiving. He even said "Father, forgive them." Jesus came to show us what sin does to us . . . how if we aren't born again we are full of selfish hate and when we separate ourselves from God we will die just like Jesus did. He also came to reveal God's love toward us so we will fall in love with him and want to be like his Son. He didn't come to earn God's

70

love for us . . .it's free . . . he already loves us."

"I don't understand, Nick. How do you know this?"

"Because I have experienced it, darling . . . I have experienced God's power in my life. My heart is overflowing with a desire to be like Him.

"I wondered what caused the wonderful changes in you. I didn't know it was Jesus." She held my face in her hands and looked at me, tears brimming in her eyes.

"You're so free and happy," she said, her voice choked with emotion. I smiled at her with tears brimming in my own eyes.

"How can I experience God's power in my life? I want what you have. You have the peace that I have been looking for, Nick . . . peace that you are accepted by God."

Her questions moved me so deeply that I couldn't answer her for some time. We had both been working so hard to earn God's love that we had become strangers in our pursuit of what we thought we had to do. Now, in one beautiful moment God was beginning to heal our lives.

"Let God change you." I said.

"How?"

"Look at who he is. Jesus showed him to us."

"He did didn't he?"

"Yes, he showed us that we don't have to earn God's love . . . it's free."

It was finally beginning to make sense. I could see it in my wife's face and I could feel it in my own heart. God was going to change us. He had shown us how through the wonderful gift of His Son. Jesus truly was a gift. I did not deserve Him, and I had not earned His love like Cain and our whole nation had tried to do. Rather, God was like Abel had understood . . . Jesus was God's free gift to us. He was God's fire from Heaven."

About the Author

Michelle Graham is the mother of two boys–Justin and Gavin–who challenge her every day to find ways to explain God's love simply enough that they, too, will love Him. They are learning in home school which provides her with a living laboratory.

Michelle hopes that you, as the reader, will find a clearer picture of God and His love for you through this book. Watch for a companion activity book to be available in your Christian bookstore, soon.

She also wrote *But Daddy, Why?* for children ages 8 - 12 who have questions about how to be good and why Jesus died. If you cannot find these books in your favorite Christian bookstore, please contact:

Rays of Hope
PO Box 336, Angwin, CA 94508
e-mail: roh@napanet.net

NOTES

NOTES

NOTES

NOTES

NOTES

How You Can Help!

If you enjoyed this book and would like to sponsor a copy or a Bible for a child in a third-world country where they do not have the money to purchase them, you can send a donation to:

PROJECT WORD
PO Box 196
Berrien Springs, MI 49103
(616) 428-4802
E-mail: skalua@projectword.org

You can find us on the internet at
www.projectword.org

Your donation of $5 can provide a Bible and this book for a child who otherwise would never have the opportunity to read them. Your donation can make a real difference in the life of a child.

WON'T YOU HELP US TELL THEM
GOD LOVES THEM, TOO?